A Gift of

The Wellesley
Free Library
Centennial Fund

Look What Came From Switzerland

by
Miles Harvey

Franklin Watts
A Division of Scholastic Inc.
New York Toronto London Auckland Sydney
Mexico City New Delhi Hong Kong
Danbury, Connecticut

Series Concept: Shari Joffe
Design: Steve Marton

Library of Congress Cataloging-in-Publication Data

Harvey, Miles.
    Look What Came From Switzerland / by Miles Harvey.
        p. cm. – (Look what came from series)
    Includes bibliographical references and index.
    Summary: Describes many things that originally came from
Switzerland, including inventions, food, animals, sports,
transportation, and medicine.
    ISBN 0-531-11963-7 (lib. bdg.) 0-531-16630-9 (pbk.)
        1. Switzerland–Civilization–Juvenile literature.
2. Civilization, Modern–Swiss influences–Juvenile literature.
[1. Switzerland–Civilization. 2. Civilization, Modern–Swiss
influences.] I. Title. II. Series.

DQ36 .H37 2002
949.4–dc21

                                              2001046793

Contents

Greetings from Switzerland!

The flag of Switzerland

Switzerland is not a very big country. Located in the center of the European continent, it is only about half the size of the state of South Carolina. Switzerland is also very hilly. Nearly 70 percent of its land is covered with mountain ranges, including the famous Alps.

But despite being small and mountainous, Switzerland is an incredible country. Not only does it boast one of the world's longest-lasting democracies, dating back more than 700 years, but it has also produced many of the cool things we use, foods we eat, and sports we play.

So come on! Let's check out all the amazing things that come from Switzerland!

Inventions

Woman putting in a contact lens

Shoe with Velcro straps

Velcro allows people to fasten and unfasten things very easily. In 1948, a man from Switzerland named George de Mestral invented this amazing product. He came up with the idea when he was hiking in the mountains and noticed the way some pointy seeds called burrs stuck to his clothing.

The Swiss also came up with the idea of **contact lenses.** A scientist from Switzerland created the first contact lenses in 1877. But they weren't tiny like today's contacts. Each covered an entire eyeball!

Another important invention that got its start in Switzerland was the **electric oven.** The first one of these stoves was put to use at a hotel in Bernina, Switzerland, in 1889.

Electric stove and oven from about 1910

more

The Swiss are famous for making excellent watches. In fact, a famous watch-making company in Switzerland called Rolex made the first **waterproof watch** in 1926. Rolex also perfected the **self-winding watch** in 1931.

Scuba diver checking the time on a waterproof watch

inventions

Another cool invention from Switzerland is the **Swiss army knife.** Though it may look like a normal pocketknife, it may contain everything from a screwdriver to a saw!

Modern-day self-winding watch

Swiss army knife

Before that, you had to keep twisting a little knob to make sure your watch didn't stop working.

Milk chocolate

Food

T he Swiss eat more chocolate per person than do the people of any other country in the world. Maybe that's because the chocolate made in Switzerland is so good! In fact, a Swiss inventor named Rudolphe Lindt came up with a way of making **smooth chocolate** in 1879. Before that, the texture of chocolate was so gritty it was almost like eating sand.

The invention of smooth chocolate made possible delicious chocolate candies such as these.

Also in 1879, a Swiss chocolate manufacturer, Daniel Peter, created the first **milk chocolate.** He did this by combining chocolate with **powdered milk,** which had been invented by a Swiss man named Henri Nestlé in 1867. During the 1930s, the Swiss also produced the first **freeze-dried coffee.**

Early advertisement for Nestlé's powdered milk

Powdered milk made by Nestlé's in the 1950s

Freeze-dried coffee

11

more food

Swiss cheese

Everybody knows about **Swiss cheese**. But that's not the only wonderful kind of cheese that comes from Switzerland. The Swiss also make a delicious cheese called **Gruyère** (pronounced groo-YAIR).

12

Rounds of Gruyère cheese

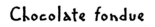
Chocolate fondue

Cheese fondue

more food

Have you ever tried **fondue?** This is Switzerland's most famous dish. To eat fondue, you put pieces of bread, meat, vegetables, or fruit on the ends of long sticks or forks. Then you dip them into bowls of melted cheese, hot oils, chocolate, or other sauces.

Raclette

Tirggel on display at a Swiss bakery

Eierzopf

Another popular Swiss dish is **raclette.** It features cheese melted over boiled potatoes. The Swiss also love baked goods, such as **eierzopf,** a kind of braided bread; and **tirggel,** a kind of sweet that's often cut into the shapes of storybook and cartoon characters.

Animals

St. Bernard

The **St. Bernard** is one of the most famous dog breeds in the world. These huge pooches come from the Swiss Alps, where they often are put to work as rescue dogs, searching for people lost in the mountains. Another kind of dog from Switzerland is the **Swiss hound.** It loves to hunt.

Swiss hound

Brown Swiss cow

Experts think the **brown Swiss cow** is one of the oldest breeds of cattle in the world. Although these animals originally came from Switzerland, they can now be found in many other places, including the United States.

Sports

No one knows exactly where ice-skating began, but the world's oldest pair of **ice skates** was found at the bottom of a lake in Switzerland. They are about 5,000 years old, and their blades are made from the leg bones of animals. In the 1800s, the sport of **mountain climbing** got its start in the Swiss Alps.

Modern-day ice skates

Also, according to some experts, the earliest organized **downhill ski race** took place in Switzerland in 1911.

Switzerland has its own unique sports, too. One of them is **stone putting.** In this event, a player must lift a huge, egg-shaped rock and try to throw it as far as possible.

A downhill ski race in Switzerland in the early 1900s

A Swiss stone putter throwing his stone

Transportation

In 1912, a Swiss company called Sulzer built the first **diesel train locomotive.** Today, diesel locomotives—which have a powerful and smooth-running type of engine—are popular around the world.

Another important transportation breakthrough was made by Auguste Piccard, a Swiss scientist living in nearby Belgium.

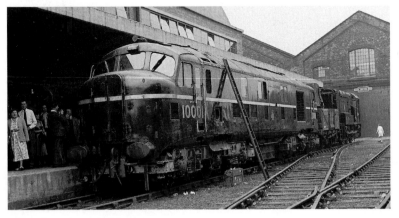

Early diesel locomotive train

During the 1930s, while attempting to build a balloon that would fly high above the clouds, Piccard came up with a great invention. He knew that the higher up you go, the less oxygen there is—and the more difficult it is to breathe. Because of this, no one had yet figured out a way to fly safely and comfortably at high altitudes. Piccard invented an **airtight cabin,** equipped with pressurized air, which gave travelers all the oxygen they needed. Today, such cabins are common on airplanes.

Modern-day pressurized airplane cabin

Piccard also designed the first **bathyscaphe** (bath-eh-SCAYF). This amazing machine allowed scientists to explore some of the deepest parts of the ocean.

Auguste Piccard's bathyscaphe in 1953

Medicine

The **International Committee of the Red Cross** is an organization that provides medical care for victims of war and other disasters. A Swiss man named Jean-Henri Dunant founded it in 1864. The group's headquarters are in the Swiss city of Geneva.

Jean-Henri Dunant

A postcard showing a Red Cross nurse and rescue dog with a wounded World War I soldier

Musical Instruments

The **Alpenhorn** is an amazing instrument. It can be as long as 20 feet (6 meters) and can be heard as far as 8 miles (13 kilometers) away! Traditionally, herders in the Alps used Alpenhorns to call cows to pasture.

Man blowing an Alpenhorn in the Swiss Alps

Children's Stories

A print from the 1800s showing the legend of William Tell

Some of the world's best-loved children's tales got their start in Switzerland. One of them is the legend of **William Tell,** who was such a good shot with a bow and arrow that he knocked an apple off the head of his own son without hurting the boy. Some people believe William Tell was a real person, but others think his story is just a myth.

JOHANNA SPYRI

Heidi grandit

FLAMMARION

The Swiss Family Robinson

PUFFIN CLASSICS

J.D. WYSS

The SWISS FAMILY ROBINSON

A book from the Heidi series by Johanna Spyri

Heidi is the famous tale of an orphan girl who lives with her grumpy old grandfather in the Swiss Alps. Johanna Spyri wrote this popular children's book in 1880.

Another beloved children's story is **The Swiss Family Robinson,** the adventures of a father, mother, and four sons who get stranded on a desert island. It was written by J. D. Wyss in 1813.

A recipe from Switzerland

A Swiss breakfast

One popular Swiss breakfast is called **Birchermüsli.** It's healthy, yummy, and easy to prepare. You can make *Birchermüsli* yourself, with the help of an adult.

To start, you'll need the following ingredients:

- 1/2 cup of uncooked, quick-cooking oatmeal
- a few pieces of your favorite fruit (such as apples, pears, or bananas)
- 2 tablespoons of wheat germ
- 3/4 to 1 cup of milk
- 1/2 cup of plain yogurt
- 1 tablespoon of honey
- optional: raisins

You'll also need the following equipment:

- a sharp knife
- a cutting board
- measuring spoons
- a measuring cup
- a wooden spoon
- a big bowl

1. Wash your hands.

2. Have an adult chop up the fruit until you get enough to fill one cup in the measuring cup.

3. Soak the uncooked oats in the milk for 1/2 hour.

4. Put the oatmeal and milk, fruit, wheat germ, yogurt, honey, and raisins into the big bowl.

5. Mix all the ingredients up with the wooden spoon.

Now you're ready to serve *Birchermüsli* to your family and friends!

How do you say....?

The majority of Swiss people speak German, but they often use different words, spellings, and pronunciations than do people in Germany. The Swiss version of German is called Swiss-German, or *Schwyzertüütsch* (SHVEET-zer-dootsch). Switzerland also has three other national languages. Many people in the western part of the country speak French. In the southeast, near the border of Italy, many people speak Italian. And in some isolated mountain valleys, people speak an ancient language called Romansch. Check out all the different ways you can say "hello" and "goodbye" when you're in Switzerland!

Language	"Hello"	How to pronounce it
German	Hallo	HAH-loh
Swiss-German	Grüezi	GROOT-zee
French	Allô	AH-loh
Italian	Ciao	chow
Romansch	Allegra	Ah-LAY-grah

Language	"Goodbye"	How to pronounce it
German	Auf Wiedersehen	owf VEE-der-zay-en
Swiss-German	Uf Widerluege	oof VEE-deer-loo-eg-uh
French	Au revoir	ah-VWAH
Italian	Arrivederci	ah-reev-uh-DEHR-chee
Romansch	Sin seveser	sin seh-veh-SEHR

To find out more

Here are some other resources to help you learn more about Switzerland:

Books

Harris, Pamela K., and Clemmons, Brad. **Switzerland** (Faces and Places series). Child's World, 2002.

Levy, Patricia, and Levy, Marjorie. **Switzerland** (Cultures of the World series). Benchmark Press, 1994.

McKay, Susan, **Switzerland** (Festivals of the World series). Gareth Stevens, 1999.

Rogers, Lura. **Switzerland** (Enchantment of the World series). Children's Press, 2001.

Organizations and Online Sites

Switzerland for Kids
http://www.eda.admin.ch/washingtn _emb/e/home/swikid.html
On this site, produced by the Swiss Embassy, you can learn how kids in Switzerland live; find out about their culture, climate, history, and food; and get answers to your questions about Switzerland.

Switzerland: A Brief Guide
http://www.admin.ch/ch/e/schweiz/ index.html
Learn the Swiss national anthem in four different languages and find out about the country's people, places, plants, and animals.

Switzerland in Sight
http://www.switzerland-in-sight.ch/ gate/index_flash.htm
This site, produced with the assistance of Swiss Radio International, is packed with useful information about Switzerland.

Flags of Switzerland
http://www.fotw.stm.it/flags/ch.html
See the Swiss flag, as well as those of the country's different states, which are known as cantons.

Map of Switzerland
http://www.lib.utexas.edu/maps/europ e/switzerland_pol_2000.jpg
Check out this online map of Switzerland, provided by the University of Texas at Austin.

Glossary

bathyscaphe a water vehicle with a watertight cabin that allows deep-sea exploration

breakthrough a sudden advance in knowledge

breed a group of animals or plants that come from common ancestors and are visibly similar in most ways

continent one of the major land masses of Earth

democracy government that is run by the people, either directly or through representatives

diesel a type of engine that works by injecting burning oil into hot, compressed air

freeze-dried coffee instant coffee powder made by removing the water content from a frozen mixture of coffee and water

legend a story coming down from the past that may or may not be true

locomotive self-propelled vehicle that runs on rails and is used for moving railroad cars

manufactured made in a factory

myth traditional story

pocketknife knife that has one or more blades that fold into the handle and can be carried in the pocket

pressurized air a special kind of oxygen that allows air travelers to breathe comfortably at high altitudes

traditional handed down from generation to generation

unique unusual; only occurring in a certain place; one of a kind

Index

Look what doesn't come from Switzerland!

Swiss steak is a cut of meat that's flattened out and then covered with tomatoes, onions, peppers and other ingredients. But Swiss steak isn't really Swiss! It may get its name from the English term "swissing," which means to roll something out.

Meet the Author

Miles Harvey is the author of several books for young people. He lives in Chicago with his wife, Rengin, and children, Azize and Julian.